First published in 2005 by Timpson Limited. © John Timpson 2006.

ISBN 0-9547049-6-7

Timpson House Claverton Road Wythenshawe Manchester M23 9TT
Tel: 0161 946 6200 www.timpson.com

Written by John Timpson CBE. Illustrated by Robert Barrow. Printed in Great Britain.

CONTENTS

Chapter One

TRAINING THE TIMPSON WAY

Why train?

Training takes a lot of money
and loads of time. Why bother?

Essential expertise

Our business depends on having people who know what they are doing.

We teach people good habits that help create the Timpson quality standard.

New superstars

A good training scheme helps to attract good quality new recruits.

Career path

Training gives us the chance to grow our own management team by always promoting from within the Company.

Never forget you were a trainee

Remember that once upon a time someone
went to the trouble to teach you.

Our future

Today's new recruits will be running
tomorrow's business.

It's easier FACE to FACE

Trainees learn much quicker from people than by reading manuals or looking at DVDs.

Everyone is a trainer

When it comes to education, everyone has a part to play – we all have a duty to help others.

How do you measure up?

Read the next few pages to discover
whether you have got what it takes
to be a training legend.

Good trainers vs bad trainers

Certain things single out the good
trainers from the bad.

Look the part

Well organised

Common sense

Chapter Two

TOP TRAINING TIPS

Here are some simple things
that make training work.

Clear plan

Think ahead and make sure each training
session is part of an overall plan.

Explain the plot

Talk through the training session before you start – telling your trainee what you hope they will achieve.

Find the time

It's easy to find an excuse for putting things off – but you must find time for training.

Never take things for granted – people are never quite the way you expect – prepare for some big surprises.

Do it your way

You don't have to follow any strict guidelines – the best trainers follow their instinct and put across their personality.

Use plain language

Use words that everyone can understand.
Don't enter the verbal Olympics – long
words don't impress anybody.

As long as he produces a good job it does not matter if the trainee uses a different method. Adapt your training to make life easy for the trainee.

Make allowances for people with learning difficulties – don't let special needs prevent people from becoming a proficient craftsman.

Teaching old dogs new tricks

Someone twenty years older than
yourself needs to be treated
differently than a teenager.

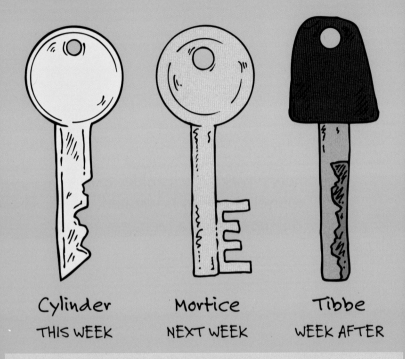

Cylinder
THIS WEEK

Mortice
NEXT WEEK

Tibbe
WEEK AFTER

Teach in small chunks

Teach a bit at a time, making sure your trainee has mastered one skill before moving on to another.

A trainee needs to do a job lots of times
before they really get the hang of it.
Everyone learns at their own pace.

TOM'S PROGRESS

IN 5 WEEKS TOM HAS CHANGED FROM A LAYABOUT TO A USEFUL MEMBER OF THE TEAM.

Give feedback

Tell your trainee how they are doing
several times every day.

Always answer questions

Answer every question sensibly and fully
– if you don't know the answer, say so.

Look out for signs of learning fatigue – there is a limit to how much people can tackle in one session. Take regular time off.

Find plenty of ways that your trainee can learn when you are not there to help. Encourage them to use the training manuals as well as talking to their colleagues.

Recap

Go back over past skills to make sure the last lesson has been truly learned before teaching something new.

Give encouragement

To make learning a positive experience, regularly point out success. Everyone needs to be told they are successful.

Recognise effort

Even when your trainee falls short of perfection, it's important to praise the effort that has been made.

Before giving an opinion ask your trainee
how they think they have done.

People are more likely to learn if they enjoy themselves. Fun is an important part of the experience.

Add to the fun by turning learning into a competition.

Lifeskills

You are not just training potential skills,
Personal behaviour is a critical part of
any training course.

Something to celebrate your first through sole repair!

Small rewards

Mark special events with a small prize.
You decide what to give and when

Workplace skills

Teach your new recruits how to be part of the team. They need to learn how to work with other people.

Make sure your trainee sticks
to our personal disciplines.

Never walk past a problem. Every time you let someone get away with something, you make matters worse.

Serious talk

If things are going wrong, have a more formal consultation. Your trainee must understand that this is serious.

If it becomes clear that your trainee will never learn, it's time to call in your Area Manager.

Push the superstars

If you have a star pupil, teach them at their pace – you will be amazed how quickly they can learn.

Agree target and practice

Make sure your trainee knows what they need to keep practising and agree some targets.

Chapter Three

HANDLING AWKWARD
SITUATIONS

Too busy to train

If the branch is very busy, help clear the back-log and leave the training until later.

If you are facing resistance, explain the benefits of the training. If you still can't win them round, stop the training and tell your A.M. you're doing so.

Take the trainee for a quiet chat and ask if you can help. Ask questions like: 'Is there anything on your mind?' 'Are you happy in your job?' 'How can we help you get back on track?'

Put them at their ease - assure them you will give all the help they need.

Chapter Four

RUNNING A COURSE

In the classroom

It is very different training people conference style, you need the experience and confidence to be good on your feet.

Check the venue

Make sure your venue is big enough,
quiet, comfortable and easy get to.

Feed the masses

Think how you can provide food and
drink during the day.

Give explicit details

Make sure everyone has plenty of notice and leave nothing to chance. If in doubt, ring up your trainees to make sure they know where to go and how to get there

Arrive early

Give yourself loads of time to get ready.

CHECKLIST
projector
lights
tea/coffee
sandwiches
no. of chairs
fire exit
pencils & paper
handouts
powerpoint

Check everything

Check you have everything ready and that everything works.

Words of welcome

Get everyone to say who they are and where they come from. It won't set the room alight, but it will get you started.

Set the rules

Rule setting is boring, but necessary, so do it at the start –everyone needs to know the guidelines.

Give reason for training

Make sure everyone knows what you are trying to achieve – make it a training day, with a purpose.

Time table

Give full details of the day ahead – let people know when they can expect a break.

Ice breaker

Grab everyone's attention with a bit of fun –
usually a quiz – to add to the enjoyment,
present some prizes.

Vary your presentation

Don't stand and talk for hour after hour, keep everyone on their toes by finding different ways to get your message across.

Flip chart

Flipcharts can help you lead
a group discussion.

Role play

It helps to act out some techniques but be careful, many people are embarrassed by role play, so wait until fairly late in the day and ask for volunteers (try to persuade everyone to have a go).

Play games

Keep the fun going by putting your points across through a game

Know your material

Practise your material, so you don't have to read the course notes. If necessary, use small cards as prompters.

Focus on the same thing as your attendees.
Don't wander behind the TV - this
will distract them!

Command your audience

Speak with an audible, confident voice.

Avoid nervous habits such as jangling the change in your pocket or using unnecessary words and phrases to stall for time.

Videos and DVDs

The Company has a library of training videos –
these may help your training session.

Problems with powerpoint

These days it is easy to create your own screen presentation but be warned, poor PowerPoint presentations can send audiences to sleep.

Don't use words...

...use pictures

Pick the tricky people

It should not take you long to spot the people who will be too loud or too quiet.

MR AWKWARD

MRS MOUSE

Your objective

Take personal pride in controlling
load mouths and getting even
the quietest to contribute.

Involve the audience

Talk with people - not at them.
Tailor the course to your participants.

Good timekeeping

Keep to your timetable - never run late.

Beware of boredom

If you see signs that you are losing
your audience - take a break.
Don't soldier on against a
room full of yawns.

Deal with disruptions

If you have someone disrupting the course, talk to them quietly during a break and point out what they are doing. If necessary send them back to their branch.

Recap

End the day by picking out the main points from the course. Remind everyone of the purpose of getting together.

MY VERDICT

Did you enjoy it? ....

....

....

....

What did you learn? ......

....

....

....

....

....

Opinion poll

Always ask for the frank feedback of
all your participants.

Nothing new
Boring
Waste of time
Dry sandwiches
Hot room

Brilliant
Learnt a lot
Good crowd
Lots of fun
Can't wait for
next one

Study results

Take a realistic look at the comments and learn how you can improve your next presentation.

The good, the bad and the...

Don't expect every attendee to be perfect. Here are some of the tricky characters you could come across.

Monopolising Mary

NOTES

Wait until she draws breath before slowing
her down with a tough question – then jump
in and ask the group to comment.

Whispering Willy

He mutters behind your back. Stop him disrupting your training session with a direct challenge. Wait until he looks at you, get him to share the comment, then ask his permission for you to continue. Sarcasm usually works with Willy.

Silent Sarah

If she is timid, refer to her by name and ask an easy question. If she is bored and balshy, ask a tough question to stop her complacency, your job is to get her involved.

He tries to make your training session his soapbox, Don't argue, he won't let you win – get the other delegates to give their views – they will be keen to shout him down.

Impulsive Irene

Keen to jump up with both feet. Slow her down and make sure she knows what she has let herself in for.

Careful Charlie

A perfectionist who gets disheartened by any mistakes. Be patient and give lots of encouragement.

Decisive Doreen

Doreen is a very quick learner – too quick –
you need to check everything she does
because she doesn't always listen to advice.

Chapter Five

SKILLS TESTING
THE TIMPSON WAY

Testing you can trust

Every trainee should have a goal and be rewarded with a qualification, but make sure the accolade is truly deserved.

Some qualifications are easy to obtain – as long as you know the systems and satisfy the red tape. Avoid tests that let passengers gain a pass.

Make sure your testing system measures the ability to do the job – not just the ability to take tests.

Be fair

Never be tempted by favouritism – the only testing system that works is scrupulously fair.

Be flexible

As long as you are testing true ability, you can break the rules. A verbal test is just as good as a written paper.

No one is a failure – but the test may indicate
when more work needs doing – it's your
job to help them pass next time.

If you are assessing a candidate who is short of skills, stop the test and train them - it's a better use of time and they'll probably be relieved.

PASS

Congratulate them, upgrade their certificate, get a picture in your Area newsletter and encourage them to go for the next level.

Pride in performance.

Make sure our skill tests are worthy of the name.
Give our people pride in a good performance.

Training is our most important investment.